Mystery at the Museum

Happy House

About Wise & Wide

- A systematic 6-level English reading program based on Lexile® measures
- Diverse and interesting topics chosen from the elementary curriculums of Korea and English speaking western countries
- Well-written books in various forms including fiction stories, descriptive texts, and classics retold
- The informative but original fiction stories grab your interest, leading to the easy and clear understanding of the educational content.
- Improve thinking skills with solid after-reading activities at all levels of the series.

Wise & Wide is a 6-level English reading program that consists of 60 books and each level is systematically divided by Lexile® measures. The Lexile® Framework for Reading is the most popular reading measuring system in American formal education curriculums and many English programs. Over 20 out of 50 states in the U.S. mark Lexile® measures directly on students' final report cards and over 300 well-known publishers adopt and use Lexile® measures.

Experience many kinds of readings written by professional writers from the U.S. and England. They used interesting topics that were carefully chosen after analyzing elementary curriculums from around the world including Korea, the U.S., England, and Australia among many others. Comprehensive after-reading activities including graphic organizers, speaking tasks, and After-reading Tests are ready for you.

Levels in the series and their corresponding Lexile® measures

Level	Lexile® measures	U.S. Grade
Level 1	Below 200L	Pre K - K
Level 2	190L - 400L	Lower Grade 1
Level 3	350L - 530L	Upper Grade 1
Level 4	420L - 650L	Grade 2
Level 5	520L - 940L	Grade 3 - 4
Level 6	830L - 1070L	Grade 5 - 6

* Smart Readers: Wise & Wide level 1 is applicable to the preschool level in the U.S.
* The source of the relationship between Lexile® measures and U.S. school grades: CCSS(Common Core State Standards) FOR ENGLISH LANGUAGE ARTS, APPENDIX A (2012, which is used by 45 states in the U.S.)

Topic List

	Level 1	Level 2	Level 3	Level 4	Level 5	Level 6
Book 1	Science>Biology: The hibernation of animals Story	Science>Biology: Living and nonliving things Story	Science>Biology> Animals & the Environment: Sea otters Story	Environment> Living with nature: The diver & the persimmon tree Story	Science>Biology> Animal: Amazing animals of the Amazon Story	Science>Biology: Germs, transmitted diseases Story
Book 2	Literature> World classics: Aesop's fables Story	Literature> Traditional fairy tale: Old tales about stones Story	Social Studies> Economy: To run a business to make and save money Story	Science>Biology> Plants: Photosynthesis Story	Science>Earth science: Earth's layers, earthquakes, volcanoes, and earth's atmosphere Report	Mathematics> Sequence: The golden ratio & the Fibonacci sequence Story
Book 3	Science>Physics: How shadows are formed Story	Literature> World classics: Peter Pan Story	Science>Scientific technology: Nanobots Story	Literature>Myths: World's creation stories Story	Literature> Legend: The story of King Arthur Story	Literature>Myths: Constellation myths Story
Book 4	Literature> Traditional literature: The Talmud Story	Science>Biology> Animal: Polar bears Story	Science>Biology> Animal: Mountain gorillas Story	Social Studies> Cultural anthropology: Amazing ancient cultures of the world Story	Science> Earth science: Clouds and weather Story	Literature> Human & animals: The friendship between a girl and a horse Story
Book 5	Social Studies> Ethics: Rules in daily life Story	Science>Biology: The five senses Report	Social Studies> Cultural anthropology: Astonishing festivals Report	Art>Music: Stories from two operas Story	Social Studies> World culture & history: The Renaissance Story	
Book 6	Social Studies> World geography & travel: Tourist attractions around the world Story	Science>Biology> Animal: Dinosaurs Story	Science> Astronomy: The solar system Story	Social Studies> People: Three great people who overcame hardships Story	Science>Scientific technology: The wonderful world of robots Report	
Book 7		Social Studies> Cultural anthropology: Mythological monsters from around the world Report		Science & Social Studies> Technology & culture: Inventions from around the world Report	Art>Works of art: Famous paintings Report	
Book 8				Social Studies> History: the California Gold Rush Report	Social Studies & Science> Psychology: Psychology in everyday life Story	
Book 9						
Book 10						

* 10 books in each level will be published.

How to Use This Book

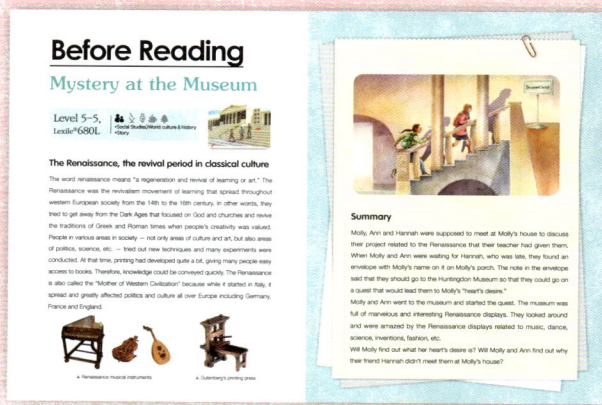

• Before Reading

You can easily find the topic and what kind of story you are about to read.

• The text

All the stories were written by professional writers from the U.S. and England, so you will read authentic and appropriate English sentences and expressions in every book in the series.

• Pop Quiz

Check out right away if you understand what you have just read by solving a pop quiz that checks your comprehension.

• Key Words

The key words and expressions on each page are listed for you to easily study them.

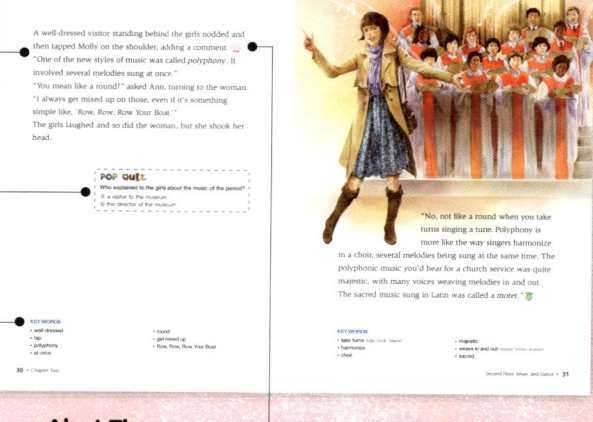

• Aha! Tips

Download free Korean explanations at *www.ihappyhouse.co.kr* for all of the sentences marked with "Aha!". These explain cultural, scientific, and economic knowledge or they deal with aspects of English such as grammatical structures or idiomatic expressions. There are lots of "Aha! Tips" to help you understand the text.

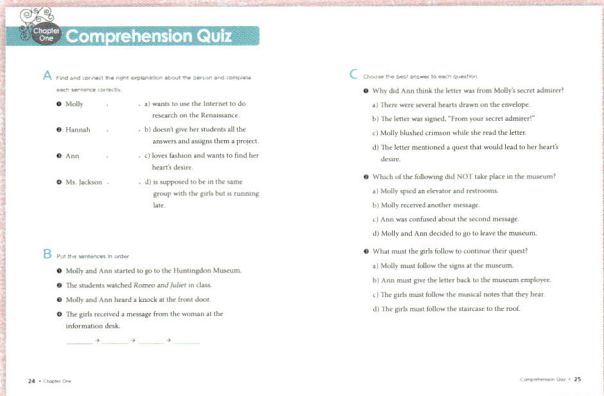

•Comprehension Quiz

After reading one chapter, solve various questions to find out if you fully understand the content.

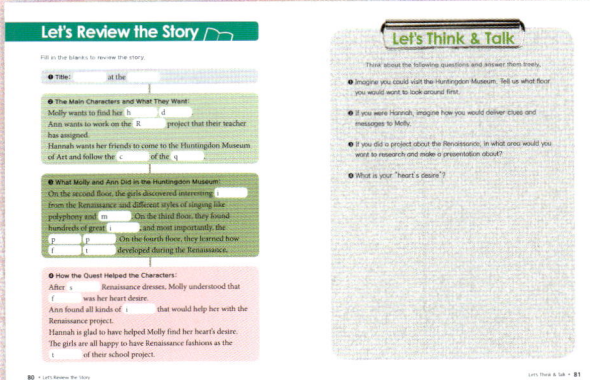

•Let's Review the Story /
•Let's Think & Talk

Fill in the blanks in the organizer to summarize the whole story. Express your own thinking and feelings about the story by answering the questions. You can build up logic and reasoning skills for your essay examinations in the future.

Appendix

Audio CD

In the CD audio book form, the texts are read vividly by American professional voice actors.

After-reading Test

Solve an additionally provided After-reading Test for each book.

The Korean translation, Answer Keys, a Word Quiz, a Word List, and Aha! Tips for each book

You can download them for free at *www.ihappyhouse.co.kr*

Before Reading

Mystery at the Museum

Level 5–5,
Lexile® 680L

•Social Studies〉World culture & history
•Story

The Renaissance, the revival period in classical culture

The word renaissance means "a regeneration and revival of learning or art." The Renaissance was the revivalism movement of learning that spread throughout western European society from the 14th to the 16th century. In other words, they tried to get away from the Dark Ages that focused on God and churches and revive the traditions of Greek and Roman times when people's creativity was valued. People in various areas in society — not only areas of culture and art, but also areas of politics, science, etc. — tried out new techniques and many experiments were conducted. At that time, printing had developed quite a bit, giving many people easy access to books. Therefore, knowledge could be conveyed quickly. The Renaissance is also called the "Mother of Western Civilization" because while it started in Italy, it spread and greatly affected politics and culture all over Europe including Germany, France and England.

▲ Renaissance musical instruments

▲ Gutenberg's printing press

Summary

Molly, Ann and Hannah were supposed to meet at Molly's house to discuss their project related to the Renaissance that their teacher had given them. When Molly and Ann were waiting for Hannah, who was late, they found an envelope with Molly's name on it on Molly's porch. The note in the envelope said that they should go to the Huntingdon Museum so that they could go on a quest that would lead them to Molly's "heart's desire."

Molly and Ann went to the museum and started the quest. The museum was full of marvelous and interesting Renaissance displays. They looked around and were amazed by the Renaissance displays related to music, dance, science, inventions, fashion, etc.

Will Molly find out what her heart's desire is? Will Molly and Ann find out why their friend Hannah didn't meet them at Molly's house?

Contents

Mystery at the Museum

Mystery at the Museum

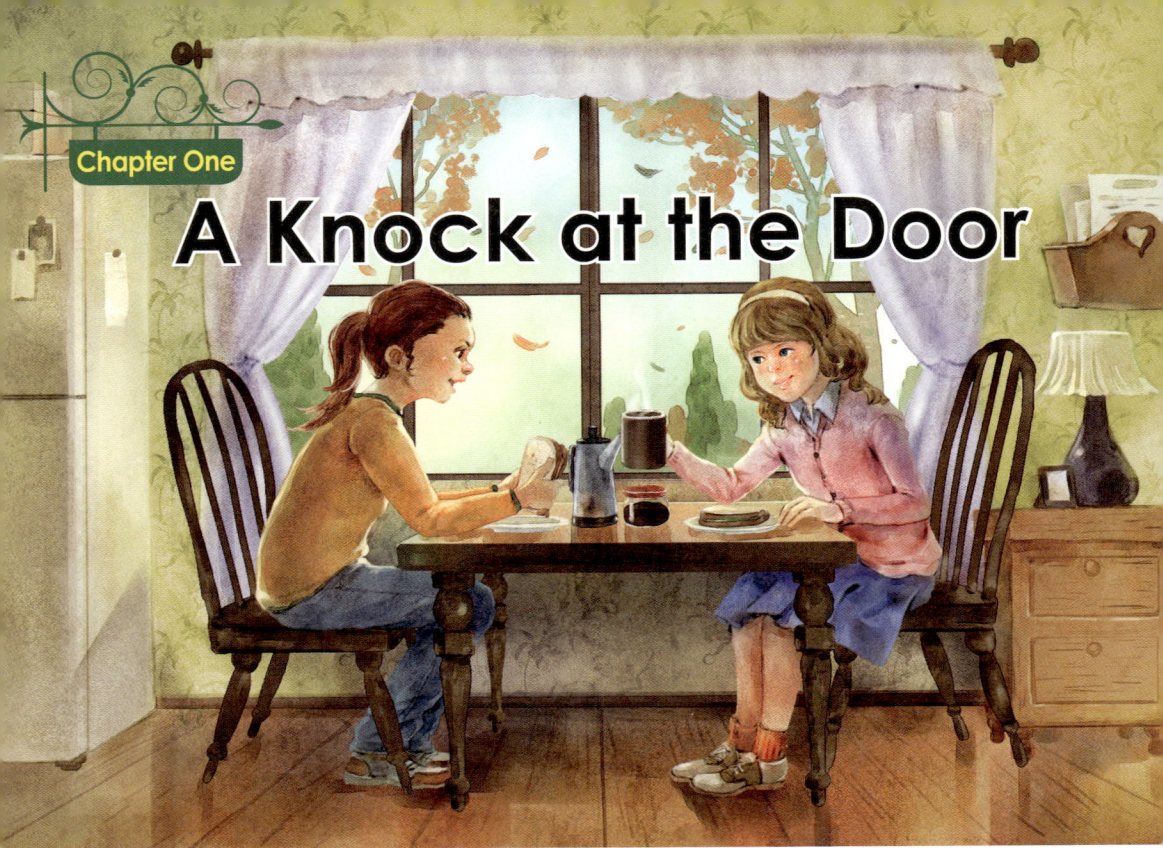

A Knock at the Door

Leaves scuttled across the sidewalk as the autumn winds whooshed in and out of trees and down the street where Molly lived. Inside, though, Molly and her friend, Ann, sat at the kitchen table, finishing a warm weekend breakfast and thinking about their plans for Saturday. So far, those plans included staying *inside* where it was snug and comfortable!

KEY WORDS

- scuttle
- sidewalk
- whoosh
- plan

- so far (= up to now)
- include
- snug
- comfortable

"When do you want to work on our project?" asked Ann. "I don't know much at all about the Renaissance. But I suppose we can look it up on the Internet."

"Oh, there's time for the project later…" Molly sipped her hot drink, lost in her thoughts. "Wasn't that a great movie yesterday?"

The girls had watched a scene from *Romeo and Juliet* at school and Molly couldn't get it out of her head. "I just love the fashions from the Renaissance period. Remember the gown Juliet wore?" Molly sighed dreamily.

POP QUIZ

What does Molly love about the movie *Romeo and Juliet*?
ⓐ the music
ⓑ the clothing

KEY WORDS

- project
- suppose
- look up
- sip
- lost in
- get A out of one's head
  (get-got-gotten[got])
- period
- gown
- wear (wear-wore-worn)
- sigh
- dreamily

"I remember that Ms. Jackson said the project was due in two weeks," said Ann.

Ms. Jackson was their teacher, and she answered questions about the Renaissance after the class had watched a short clip from the movie. But she was not the kind of teacher who would tell her students *all* the answers. So the class was given an assignment: to investigate the Renaissance period and find something interesting to share.

Ann and Molly were in a group with their friend, Hannah, and they were meeting today at Molly's house to talk about the project. But Hannah was running late.

POP QUIZ

Why did Ms. Jackson assign a project to the class?
ⓐ She wanted to keep her students busy.
ⓑ She wanted her students to find answers for themselves.

KEY WORDS

- due
- clip
- assignment
- investigate
- share
- run late (run-ran-run)

Ann rinsed out her mug. "Where is Hannah, anyway? The sooner we start on this boring project, the sooner we can finish."

Molly nodded as a knock sounded at the front door. But when the girls opened the door, no one was there. All they noticed was an envelope on the top step. It had Molly's name on it.

KEY WORDS

- rinse out
- mug
- nod

- notice
- envelope
- step

"Is that from Hannah?" asked Ann. "Why did she leave?"

Molly ripped open the envelope. "It's not signed." She shrugged.

"Ooooh," said Ann. "A secret admirer?"

Molly blushed crimson! "Don't be silly." Ann peered over her shoulder while Molly read the note aloud. "You have been specially chosen for a quest, a quest that will lead you to your heart's desire!"

"Your heart's desire," said Ann. "I told you it was from a secret admirer!"

"Shhh!" Molly raised her finger and shushed her friend and then continued, her heart pounding. "If you accept, go to the Huntingdon Museum of Art where you'll find clues to aid you in your search. Do not delay! The museum is free to the public today, but you must enter before 12:00."

"How exciting!" Ann's eyes lit up. "Who could've sent you that note?"

"I don't have any idea," said Molly. "But I can't possibly pass up a quest, can I?" She wrapped a scarf around her neck and once more opened the door.

POP QUIZ

Where must the girls go to find clues for their quest?

ⓐ an art museum
ⓑ a public library

KEY WORDS

- rip open
- sign
- **shrug** (shrug-shrugged-shrugged)
- secret admirer
- blush
- crimson
- peer
- quest

- heart's desire
- shush
- pound
- clue
- aid
- delay
- **light up** (light-lit-lit)
- pass up

"What about Hannah?" asked Ann. "Should we wait for her? Besides, it's *so* cold outside!"

"We can leave a note for her and she can catch up with us. After all, I'm dying to begin the quest to find my heart's desire!" Molly grabbed her coat and handed Ann a fleece-lined jacket. "And we'll bundle up! Come on! We've got a bus to catch to the Huntingdon Museum of Art."

The girls hopped off the bus and stepped at a brisk pace until they reached the wide, double doors to the museum.

A line had formed and Molly and Ann waited their turn. Ann raised her head, counting the floors. "Four stories! This is a big museum," she said. "How are we ever going to find a clue?"

KEY WORDS

- besides
- catch up with
  (catch-caught-caught)
- after all
- be dying to

- grab
- fleece-lined
- bundle up
- hop off
- at a brisk pace

- double doors
- form
- count

"I'm not sure," said Molly. "Perhaps we'll find another note?"

The line moved forward and the girls pushed through the door at last. A simple but sweet string melody greeted them as they entered. It seemed to come from the floor above. Aha!

"What should we do now?" asked Ann.

Molly turned in a circle around the entryway. She had never been inside the Huntingdon Museum, and she was impressed by the grandeur of the old building.

POP QUIZ

What impressed Molly when she arrived at the museum?
ⓐ the simple melody that she heard
ⓑ the grandeur of the building

KEY WORDS

- perhaps
- forward
- push through
- string
- greet

- turn in a circle
- entryway
- impress
- grandeur

In the center of the main floor, a white, marble staircase led to the three floors above. Long, flowing banners, imprinted with beautiful calligraphy, spilled from the dark mahogany banisters over her head. She spied an elevator and restrooms and a gift shop, too, but she didn't think any of those areas would help her in her quest. An information desk on the left seemed like the perfect place to start looking for clues to the mystery of the message she'd received.

"I'm Molly, and this is my friend, Ann," said Molly. She felt foolish, introducing herself to the employee behind the counter. But what if a clue had been left for them?

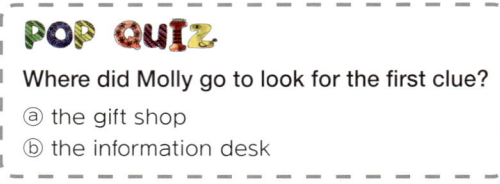

POP QUIz

Where did Molly go to look for the first clue?
ⓐ the gift shop
ⓑ the information desk

KEY WORDS

- marble
- staircase
- flowing
- banner (= placard; flag)
- imprint
- calligraphy
- spill
- mahogany
- banister (= handrail)

- spy
- mystery
- introduce oneself
- employee
- what if
- wonder if
- flustered
- as well
- puzzled

"Hello, Molly and Ann," said the young woman. "Welcome to the Huntingdon Museum of Art. How may I help you?"

"We were wondering if you had a …" Ann was not sure what to say. She looked at Molly.

"A… note," said Molly, a bit flustered as well. "Or any kind of message left for me?"

"I don't think so," said the woman, a puzzled look on her face.

But she searched the desk and counter, and then opened a drawer. She gasped and looked up. "That's strange," said the woman. "It appears I *do* have a letter for Molly, after all." She passed the envelope to the girls.

"Thank you," said Molly, a tingle of excitement zipping through her. She tore open the second envelope.

KEY WORDS

- search
- gasp
- appear

- a tingle of excitement
- zip through
- **tear open** (tear-tore-torn)

"Welcome to your quest!" read Ann from over her shoulder. "Do you like the music you hear? You can find out more about the tune on the second floor, and P.S. The musical notes might lead you to your heart's desire!" Ann paused, and raised her eyebrows. "But what does that mean?" Molly looked up the stairway. "I think we'll have to search the second floor to find out!"

KEY WORDS

- tune
- P.S. (postscript)
- musical note
- raise one's eyebrows
- stairway
- find out (find-found-found)

Comprehension Quiz

A Find and connect the right explanation about the person and complete each sentence correctly.

❶ Molly •   • a) wants to use the Internet to do research on the Renaissance.

❷ Hannah •   • b) doesn't give her students all the answers and assigns them a project.

❸ Ann •   • c) loves fashion and wants to find her heart's desire.

❹ Ms. Jackson •   • d) is supposed to be in the same group with the girls but is running late.

B Put the sentences in order.

❶ Molly and Ann started to go to the Huntingdon Museum.

❷ The students watched *Romeo and Juliet* in class.

❸ Molly and Ann heard a knock at the front door.

❹ The girls received a message from the woman at the information desk.

_____ → _____ → _____ → _____

C Choose the best answer to each question.

❶ Why did Ann think the letter was from Molly's secret admirer?

a) There were several hearts drawn on the envelope.

b) The letter was signed, "From your secret admirer!"

c) Molly blushed crimson while she read the letter.

d) The letter mentioned a quest that would lead to her heart's desire.

❷ Which of the following did NOT take place in the museum?

a) Molly spied an elevator and restrooms.

b) Molly received another message.

c) Ann was confused about the second message.

d) Molly and Ann decided to go to leave the museum.

❸ What must the girls follow to continue their quest?

a) Molly must follow the signs at the museum.

b) Ann must give the letter back to the museum employee.

c) The girls must follow the musical notes that they hear.

d) The girls must follow the staircase to the roof.

Second Floor, Music and Dance

"Oh!" This time, Molly gasped when they arrived at the second floor. "It's the Renaissance!"

Ann and Molly stood before an elaborately scripted sign, announcing the Renaissance exhibit at the Huntingdon Museum. The music seemed to drift from a point somewhere to their right.

"The music must be from a CD, playing over a speaker," said Molly.

"Is music from the Renaissance your heart's desire?" asked Ann.

"I don't think so. I don't even know much about the music from… when is the Renaissance, anyway?"

"That's a good question," said Ann. "But at least we're in the right place to find that answer." She pointed to her right, at a plaque on the wall and began to read aloud.

"The end of the Middle Ages coincided with the beginning of the Renaissance, a period that started in Florence, Italy in the 14th century and spread throughout Europe. The word Renaissance means 'rebirth' and this period is marked by changes in the way people looked at life and politics, music and dance, art and science. During medieval times, people often viewed life as a hardship, but around 1350, attitudes began to change. The Europeans who had survived the Black Plague…"

KEY WORDS

- elaborately
- script
- exhibit
- drift
- plaque
- coincide with
- rebirth

- mark
- politics
- medieval
- view A as B
- hardship
- attitude
- survive

A shiver ran down Ann's spine. "That sounds horrible, doesn't it? Anyway, it says people began to study Greek and Roman scholars and realized that in the past, people had enjoyed many of the artistic aspects life offered. So they began to create lighter music and dance as part of this cultural rebirth." 📖 Aha!

"Yes," said Molly. She read from the next plaque adjacent to a large canvas depicting men and women from the period, playing instruments and singing. "Music and dance became a part of everyday life; new instruments were invented and new styles of singing were introduced."

KEY WORDS

- **shiver** (= tremble)
- **spine**
- **scholar**
- **artistic**
- **aspect**
- **offer**

- **cultural**
- **adjacent to**
- **canvas**
- **depict**
- **instrument**
- **invent**

A well-dressed visitor standing behind the girls nodded and then tapped Molly on the shoulder, adding a comment. 📖 Aha!

"One of the new styles of music was called *polyphony*. It involved several melodies sung at once."

"You mean like a round?" asked Ann, turning to the woman. "I always get mixed up on those, even if it's something simple like, 'Row, Row, Row Your Boat.'"

The girls laughed and so did the woman, but she shook her head.

POP QUIZ

Who explained to the girls about the music of the period?

ⓐ a visitor to the museum
ⓑ the director of the museum

KEY WORDS

- well-dressed
- tap
- polyphony
- at once

- round
- get mixed up
- Row, Row, Row Your Boat

"No, not like a round when you take turns singing a tune. Polyphony is more like the way singers harmonize in a choir, several melodies being sung at the same time. The polyphonic music you'd hear for a church service was quite majestic, with many voices weaving melodies in and out. The sacred music sung in Latin was called a *motet*."

KEY WORDS

- **take turns** (take-took-taken)
- **harmonize**
- **choir**

- **majestic**
- **weave in and out** (weave-wove-woven)
- **sacred**

"Thank you," said Molly. The woman ambled over to another display, and Molly turned to Ann. "The tune we're hearing doesn't sound like majestic church music, does it?"

"No," said Ann. "It sounds like…" She paused. "You know, I think it's English!"

Ann walked to the next plaque and read. "*Madrigals* were a form of popular music that developed during the early Renaissance, and they had a polyphonic structure in which three or more singers would voice different melodies.

The text was often in the common language of the people: Italian, French or English. Madrigals were usually romantic poems put to music."

KEY WORDS

- amble
- madrigal
- polyphonic
- structure

- voice
- text
- romantic

"See?" said Ann. "It must be a madrigal. Perhaps it's some kind of romantic poem. That could be your heart's desire."
"I don't think so," replied Molly. "It's very nice, but I prefer more contemporary music. And the electric guitar."
The girls laughed and wandered over to a display of instruments. "Look at this violin," said Molly. "I didn't know the violin was first made in Italy during the Renaissance."

KEY WORDS

- prefer
- contemporary
- electric
- wander

At least they recognized that particular stringed instrument. The girls had never seen many of the instruments in the collection.  They put on headphones that were connected to the display. At each instrument, they pressed a button, listened to a tune, and read the description. "This is a harpsichord," said Molly, pressing the first button. The instrument looked like a piano. "When you play a key, it sounds like you're plucking a string!"

▲ harpsichord

POP QUIZ

Which instrument does a harpsichord look like?

ⓐ an electric guitar
ⓑ a piano

KEY WORDS

- recognize
- particular
- stringed instrument
- collection
- be connected to

- description
- harpsichord
- key
- pluck

▲ hurdy-gurdy

"This is a hurdy-gurdy." Ann pressed the next button. "Doesn't it look like a violin with an accordion on top of it? It makes music when a wheel turns and rubs against the strings."

Molly stood before the instrument next to the violin and paused. "I think I remember this instrument from when we watched *Romeo and Juliet*. One of the characters was playing it." She pressed the button on a lute, which looked similar to a guitar except that the back was rounder and deeper. 📖 Aha!

▲ lute

KEY WORDS

- hurdy-gurdy
- accordion
- rub against
- character
- lute
- similar to

"The lute's my favorite instrument of the Renaissance," said Ann.

"Mine, too, I think," said Molly.

They put the headphones back and looked around. They had reached the opposite end of the second floor, and now it seemed as if they were closer to the music that played overhead.

"The madrigal sounds as if it's just around the corner, doesn't it?" Molly pulled Ann along, and they stepped out into an old-fashioned parlor.

"Musicians!" said Ann.

"And singers!" said Molly.

A museum volunteer called a docent sat in front of the costumed group standing in the parlor. One musician was strumming a lute, and the other played a hurdy-gurdy. Four women sang a rousing melody in four-part harmony.

POP QUIZ

Who did the girls find in an old-fashioned parlor?

ⓐ musicians
ⓑ costumed visitors

KEY WORDS

- opposite
- as if
- just around the corner
- step out into

- old-fashioned
- parlor
- volunteer
- docent

- costumed
- strum
- rousing

The music stopped and the men bowed while the women curtseyed. Molly and Ann applauded. It was easy to see why the common people had enjoyed this lively music so much!

KEY WORDS

- curts(e)y
- applaud

- common people
- lively

The docent smiled. "That was a madrigal written by Jacques Arcadelt, one of the most famous and influential composers of this popular music.  His works, performed during the early period of the Renaissance, were considered classics, and the

▲ the front page of the works of madrigal composed by Jacob Arcadelt

publication of his first book of madrigals helped spread this vocal music beyond Italy to other parts of Europe."

Ann turned to Molly. "How about the music of the Renaissance for our project? I bet we could find a CD and play some songs for the class. What do you think?"

Molly shrugged. "I suppose that would be okay."

KEY WORDS

- influential
- composer
- be considered
- publication
- I bet
- fascinating

- flip through
- music
- stand
- shuffle
- beam
- indeed

It had been fascinating to learn about Renaissance music and instruments, but she was disappointed. The madrigal wasn't her heart's desire, and she had no idea where to look next.

"You don't look very excited, Molly." Ann sighed.

The lute player stood suddenly and flipped through the music on his stand. "Excuse me! One of you is Molly? I have…" He shuffled the pages.

"Ah! Here it is!" He handed Molly an envelope.

"Oh, thank you!" Molly beamed. She hadn't found her heart's desire, but the musical notes had indeed led her to another clue!

A Match each instrument with the right explanation.

❶ violin •

• a) This instrument sounds like you're plucking a string.

❷ harpsichord •

• b) A character in *Romeo and Juliet* played this instrument.

❸ hurdy-gurdy •

• c) This instrument makes music when a wheel turns.

❹ lute •

• d) Molly and Ann recognized this stringed instrument.

B Mark T for true or F for false.

❶ The Asians who had survived the Black Plague influenced the Renaissance. T F

❷ The Renaissance was marked by changes in the way people looked at life. T F

❸ Music and dance were not a part of everyday life during the Renaissance. T F

❹ New styles of singing were introduced during the Renaissance. T F

C Choose the best answer to each question.

❶ Which of the following statements about madrigals is NOT true?

a) Madrigals were a form of popular music.

b) Madrigals did not develop until the end of the Renaissance.

c) Three or four singers would voice different melodies.

d) The text was often in the common language of the people.

❷ Where did the girls finally catch up to the madrigal music?

a) at the entryway of the second floor

b) on a stage on the second floor

c) in an old-fashioned parlor on the second floor

d) in a concert hall on the third floor

❸ Why did Ann think that music would be a fun Renaissance project?

a) The girls could bring the instruments to show the class.

b) The girls could introduce a madrigal to the class and sing it together.

c) The girls could bring a CD of Renaissance music and play it for the class.

d) The girls could take the class to the museum so that they could enjoy the music.

Third Floor, Science and Inventions

"What does it say?" Ann nudged Molly to read the letter. "It says, 'People experimented with music and instruments during the Renaissance, but they also applied their *scientific thinking* to other aspects of daily life. Keep searching if you want to find your heart's desire!'"

"The next floor is Inventions," said Ann. "That's scientific thinking, I guess. Do you have a favorite invention? One that would be your heart's desire?"

Invention

Molly shook her head no. "I don't care much for science, but we have to keep searching if we're ever going to figure out this riddle."

The girls raced up the next set of stairs to the third floor. When they reached the entrance into this gallery, their eyes widened with surprise. There were inventions, of course, but there were also scale models of buildings and drawings of the human anatomy. The Renaissance exploded with scientific discovery!

▲ a Renaissance building

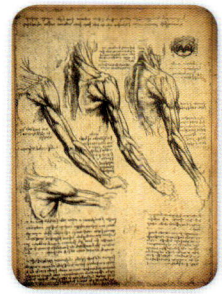
▲ a Renaissance anatomical chart

KEY WORDS

- nudge
- experiment
- apply
- scientific
- care for

- keep + *Verb*-ing
- figure out
- race (= run)
- widen
- scale model

- human anatomy
- explode
- discovery

▲ Filippo Brunelleschi

Molly read the first plaque: "Art and science came together during the Renaissance as people began to study the world around them. To create statues, artists studied the human body. To design new buildings, architects like Filippo Brunelleschi studied math. And that was just the beginning…"

"So where shall we start?"

"Oh, I recognize this invention," said Molly. "It's the printing press! Let's start there."

Ann read a scroll with medieval-looking print. "Johannes Gutenberg was a German inventor who revolutionized the written word with his printing press."

▲ Gutenberg's printing press

KEY WORDS

- **come together** (come-came-come)
- **architect**
- **printing press**
- **scroll**
- **revolutionize**
- **recess**
- **inviting**

- **patron**
- **at work**
- **labor-intensive**
- **improvement**
- **moveable[movable] type**
- **set up** (set-set-set)

A video screen, recessed in the wall, looked inviting.
The girls sat on a bench with several other patrons. A young
boy pressed the button so they could watch a film of a
printing press at work. They learned that making books had
been a slow and labor-intensive process before 1440.
But Gutenberg added improvements like *moveable type* so
that pages could be set up much more quickly. Aha!

He found a way to print pages faster, too; his press could print thousands of pages per day rather than just the 40 to 50 pages that had been produced before. Because books could be printed so rapidly and were less costly, the written word spread throughout Europe, even to those commoners in the middle classes. By 1500, there were more printing presses and this feat allowed for the spread of other scientific discoveries.

KEY WORDS

- rapidly
- costly
- commoner
- middle class
- feat

"Wow," said Molly. "The printing press really made a difference in people's lives, didn't it? It was like the Internet of the Renaissance!" "And look," said Ann. "Here's a page from the famous Gutenberg Bible." She read the information beside the glass-enclosed page. "Before Gutenberg's press, bibles were hard to come by. It could take a year or more for a bible

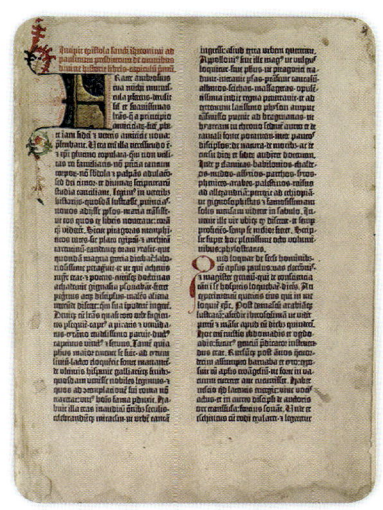

▲ a page in Gutenberg's bible

to be transcribed. Gutenberg produced 200 bibles that were available to a wider audience. A Gutenberg Bible may have cost about 30 florins during the Renaissance. But today, that same bible is worth 30 million dollars! There are about 20 Gutenberg Bibles thought to be in existence today."

POP QUIZ

How many bibles did Gutenberg produce using his press?
ⓐ 20 bibles
ⓑ 200 bibles

KEY WORDS

- make a difference
  (make-made-made)
- glass-enclosed
- come by
- transcribe
- available
- audience
- cost (cost-cost-cost)
- florin
- be in existence

"If only I had a Gutenberg Bible," said Molly with a sigh.
"I'd be rich!"

"That must be your heart's desire!" exclaimed Ann.

"No," said Molly. "Money is helpful, but it's not my heart's desire."

They walked to the other side of the room where they found a display of other Renaissance inventions. They looked through a microscope and a telescope and read about eyeglasses.

"Gosh, it must have been hard for people to read before eyeglasses were invented," said Ann. "It's a good thing they made so many improvements to *lenses.*"

"It's a good thing they had the *Scientific Method.*" Molly pointed to a display that listed the steps. "I remember those steps. We used them when we worked on our science fair project. It says that during the Renaissance, the scientific method was further developed. Galileo performed controlled experiments and analyzed data."

▲ Galileo

POP QUIZ

What inventions were related to improvements in lenses?

ⓐ books and the printing press
ⓑ the microscope and the telescope

KEY WORDS

- exclaim
- look through
- microscope
- telescope
- eyeglasses (= glasses)
- gosh
- scientific method
- list
- science fair
- controlled experiment
- analyze

▲ a Renaissance grandfather clock

"And look! Here's another fact about Galileo." Molly walked to a tall, grandfather-style clock and scanned the information provided on a card nearby. "He helped keep people on time! It says here that in 1581, he invented the *pendulum* which made clocks much more accurate."

"But I thought Galileo was all about astronomy," said Ann. "Didn't he invent the telescope?"

Molly and Ann walked over to a timeline that ran the length of an entire wall, detailing events from Galileo's life.

"He didn't invent it," said Molly, skimming the information. "But he improved it so that he could see the planets and observe them."

POP QUIZ

Why was Galileo arrested?
ⓐ He believed the Earth was the center of the universe.
ⓑ He wrote the Earth rotated around the sun.

KEY WORDS

- grandfather-style
- scan
- provide
- on time
- pendulum

- accurate
- astronomy
- timeline
- run
- detail

- skim
- planet
- observe

She began to read from a section under the year 1632. "Like Copernicus, another famous astronomer, Galileo believed that the planets, including the Earth, rotated around the sun. He wrote a book about his theories called *The Dialogue Concerning the Two Chief World Systems.*"

"Uh-oh," said Ann. "It says he was arrested for writing about that scientific discovery! During the Renaissance, people believed that the Earth was the center of the universe. But good for Galileo, sticking to his beliefs," said Ann, proudly. "He followed what he knew to be true! I guess science was *his* heart's desire!"

KEY WORDS

- section
- astronomer
- rotate

- theory
- world system
- be arrested for

- universe
- stick to (stick-stuck-stuck)

Molly nodded and sighed again. They had explored the entire third floor and she still hadn't found *her* heart's desire. But at the last exhibit, she couldn't help smiling. "Look," she said. "Two essential tools of every workman, the screwdriver and wrench, were invented during the Renaissance.

▲ a Renaissance flushing toilet

And flushing toilets! I'm sure people were happy about that last invention!"

"Oh, Molly!" Ann laughed and pulled her friend's arm. "Where shall we go next?"

POP QUIZ

What essential tools used by workmen today were invented during the Renaissance?

ⓐ the screwdriver and wrench
ⓑ flushing toilets and the printing press

KEY WORDS

- explore
- can't help + *Verb*-ing
- essential
- workman
- screwdriver
- wrench
- flushing toilet

Molly paused and surveyed the rooms. There were no musicians this time around to hand out another envelope. She couldn't even find a docent! But she was sure there was a message for her, somewhere on the third floor. But where, she wondered. They had walked in a circle through the rooms and were right back where they started from—at the printing press.

KEY WORDS

- survey   - hand out

"Oh! The printing press!" said Molly. If someone wanted to leave a message, she thought, a printing press would come in handy. "Wasn't there a demonstration of how it worked? You could print your own message, right?"

"You want to print a message? Now?" asked Ann.

"Not exactly. I want to see if a message was printed and left for *us*!"

The girls found the desk where the equipment was set up. A crowd of young children was busily setting type to print a message.

Above the press was a bulletin board where some people had posted their printed texts for other visitors to see. There, in big block letters, was a note addressed to Molly!

"You were right!" said Ann. She pulled the note off the board and began to read it aloud.

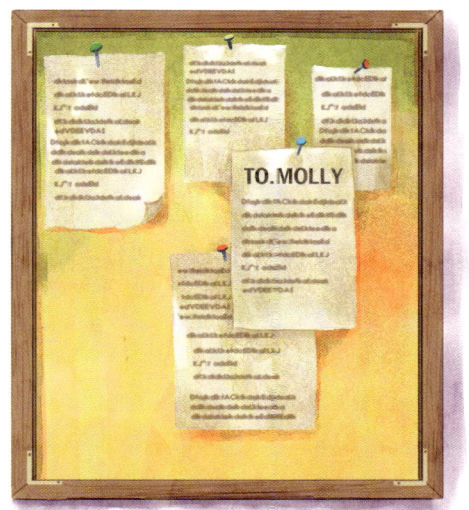

TO.MOLLY

POP QUIZ

What invention led the girls to the next clue?
ⓐ the flushing toilet
ⓑ the printing press

KEY WORDS

- come in handy
- demonstration
- equipment
- set type
- bulletin board

- post
- block letter
- address
- pull off

A Mark T for true or F for false.

❶ Many important inventions were made during the
Renaissance. T F

❷ When the girls reached the third floor, they were
disappointed. T F

❸ The girls explored religious thinking on the third floor. T F

B Find and connect the right explanation about the person and complete
each sentence correctly.

❶ Brunelleschi •   • a) improved printing.

❷ Galileo   •   • b) studied math to design buildings.

❸ Gutenberg   •   • c) invented the pendulum.

C Fill in each blank with the right word below to complete each sentence
according to the story.

experiments	labor-intensive	scientific

❶ Before 1440 making books had been a _____ process.

❷ During the Renaissance the _____ method was further
developed.

❸ Galileo performed controlled _____ and analyzed data.

D Choose the best answer to each question.

❶ Which of the following inventions did the girls NOT find on
the third floor?

a) drawings and statues of the human body

b) eyeglasses, the microscope, and the telescope

c) the printing press and a page of the Gutenberg Bible

d) the screwdriver and the wrench, and flushing toilets

❷ Which of the following statements about Galileo is NOT true?

a) He helped keep people on time.

b) He improved the telescope.

c) He believed the planets rotated around the sun.

d) He was free to discuss his scientific beliefs.

❸ Why did Molly think the printing press might lead her to the
next clue?

a) It was the first invention she saw when she arrived on the
third floor.

b) She was sure Gutenberg had left a message for her.

c) She thought a printing press would come in handy for writing
a message.

d) A docent told her it would be a good place to look for the clue.

Fourth Floor, Fashions

Clothing of the Renaissance

"The printing press was instrumental in bringing information to the masses in Europe, and just like the Hollywood gossip magazines today, fashion trends spread quickly through the written word. Perhaps your heart's desire will be threaded with silver and gold!"

"Let's see…" Molly tapped her index finger against her chin. "Fashion trends and gossip magazines… threaded with silver and gold…" She snapped her fingers. "I've got it!  On to the next floor. It's Clothing of the Renaissance."

"I sure hope you find your heart's desire there," said Ann. "The next floor is the *last* floor!"

Molly arrived at the entryway to the fourth floor first. A docent greeted her.

POP QUIZ

How did fashion trends quickly spread in Europe?
ⓐ through the written word
ⓑ through gossip and paintings

KEY WORDS

- instrumental
- masses
- gossip
- fashion trend

- be threaded with
- snap one's fingers
- sure

"Good morning," she said. "We have quite a few pieces of clothes on display here, and please…" she paused as Ann joined her. "Feel free to touch!"

"Well, that's different," said Ann. "Usually in a museum, you're not allowed to touch anything!"

Molly made a beeline to a long row of mannequins. "I think these costumes are recreations of Renaissance designs. That explains why you're allowed to touch the fabrics. Oh! Feel this fur," she said, running a finger down a dress. "Aren't these dresses beautiful?"

Ann pointed to an area that looked like a movie theater. "Wait a minute." She looked at the screen on the wall where a movie was playing. "Isn't that the same movie we watched in class yesterday? I recognize the actors who played Romeo and Juliet."

"I recognize Juliet's *dress*," said Molly. Her face lit up. "And Romeo's clothes, too. I wonder if everyone dressed like that during the 1400's…"

KEY WORDS

- quite a few
- feel free to + *Verb*
- make a beeline to

- mannequin
- recreation
- fabrics

- fur
- dress

Ann read a plaque while Molly pulled out a notebook and a pencil. "Fashion was an important part of Renaissance life. The wealthy used clothing to establish their position in society. 📖 They spent large amounts of money, copying the latest styles. Furs, fine silks, even threads of silver and gold were used in many of the designs, and not just for women."

POP QUIZ

Why did the wealthy spend a lot on clothing during the Renaissance?

ⓐ They became rich by making art and fashion.
ⓑ They wanted to establish their position in society.

KEY WORDS

- establish
- position
- copy
- latest
- thread

"Silver and gold thread," said Molly. "I knew it! Look at the embroidery work on this dress." Admiring the dressmaker's skills with a needle, she opened her notebook and began to sketch the dress in front of her. "Keep reading," she said. "I don't want to miss anything, but I want to get as many of these fashions sketched out as I can."

"Okay, let's see…" Ann walked over to a male mannequin and began to read. "Men wore colorful stockings or tights to show off their legs, and a shirt and tunic or coat. The coat was generally tight-fitting and called a *doublet.*"

"Yes, like Romeo wore."

"Exactly. And in the early Renaissance period, women wore long dresses, with high waists and puffy sleeves. 'A well-to-do Renaissance woman most likely had an entire collection of fine dresses while a peasant likely owned only one set of clothes.' I wouldn't like that. Think of how often you'd have to do laundry!"

POP QUIZ

What items did women wear during the Renaissance?
ⓐ colorful stockings and doublets
ⓑ long dresses with high waists

KEY WORDS

- embroidery
- admire
- dressmaker
- miss
- sketch out
- tights
- show off (show-showed-showed[shown])
- tunic
- tight-fitting

- doublet
- high waist
- puffy
- well-to-do
- likely
- peasant
- own
- do laundry

"Oh, I don't think they washed their clothes very often," said Molly. She paused, her pencil was still for a change. "Listen to this: People rarely bathed. It was common for men and women to wear heavy perfumes which not only masked the odors in the streets but also the smell of clothing that might be cleaned only a couple times a year, as well as a body that might be washed once in a month's time."

"Ewww," said the girls.

Molly walked to the next group of mannequins. "The styles have changed here. Could you keep reading? I want to sketch one of these dresses."

POP QUIZ

Why did Ann keep reading the plaques about fashion to Molly?

ⓐ Molly preferred to touch and feel the clothing.
ⓑ Molly was busy sketching the fashion designs.

KEY WORDS

- still
- for a change
- rarely
- perfume

- not only A but also B (= B as well as A)
- mask
- odor
- ewww

Ann nodded. "As the Renaissance continued, styles were influenced by the monarchs. By the end of Elizabeth's reign, waistlines dropped, eventually forming a deep V, and women wore barrel-shaped petticoats called a *farthingale*, which gave a hooped shape to the skirts." Ann giggled. "Here's something funny. 'The farthingales grew bigger and bigger, requiring so much material, that laws were made to limit them.  But everyone just ignored the laws.'"

▲ Elizabeth I

Molly laughed. "It's not a good idea to tell women what they can and cannot wear." She looked at the faces of the women. "Do you think they look pale? Renaissance ladies would have fit in nicely in a vampire movie!"

"You really have a keen eye for details," said Ann. She read the plaque. "A white complexion was dearly valued, so women wore veils or hats to keep their skin from getting any sun."

Molly put the finishing touches on her sketch and read the next plaque. She'd noticed that the women had unusually large foreheads, too, and now she knew why. "Listen, Ann. 'Women would pluck their hairline on the forehead, and sometimes their eyebrows, too, to give the appearance of a high forehead.' That's odd, isn't it?"

A docent wandered over, smiling. "It's not really odd when you realize that during this time, people believed a high forehead signified intelligence. And intelligence was highly valued during the Renaissance."

POP QUIZ

What did a high forehead signify during the Renaissance?

ⓐ intelligence
ⓑ elegance

KEY WORDS

- pale
- fit in
- vampire
- have a keen eye for
- complexion
- dearly
- value

- veil
- put a finishing touch on
- hairline
- high forehead
- odd
- signify
- intelligence

She continued, "Think of all those great minds, like Galileo and Gutenberg, Michelangelo and Shakespeare. Knowledge was the light that brought the people out of the Dark Ages, and all of those scientists and inventors and artists and poets were… well, they were the rock stars of the Renaissance! 🌐 Everyone wanted to be like them. It was a very exciting time in history, girls."

▲ Michelangelo

▲ Shakespeare

KEY WORDS

- **mind** (= intelligent person) (*cf.* great minds)
- **afford**
- **court** (= palace)

- **ball**
- **elegant**

Molly nodded. "I imagine it was more exciting for those who were wealthy, for women who could afford these amazing fashions! I would have loved to go to a dance at a court ball, wearing one of these elegant dresses. I know just what I'd wear, too. Here," she said, showing Ann the page where she'd sketched the golden-threaded dress. "That's my favorite style of all the dresses."

"Oh, this is beautiful," whispered Ann, studying the design. "I didn't know you could draw this well."

"Do you like it? I've been practicing a little, sketching fashion designs. This Renaissance exhibit has inspired my inner artist!"

The docent leaned over Molly's shoulder, looking at her sketches. "What lovely sketches!"

Molly blushed while Ann nodded.

"You girls might enjoy the display at the other end of the room," she said, pointing. "It's life-sized figures of a man and woman in typical Renaissance garb."

"Thanks," said Molly and they walked across the room.

"Look! The faces are cut out so you can take a picture of yourself as a Renaissance woman." Ann smiled. "You go first."

Molly stood behind the figure of the woman and poked her face through the hole.

POP QUIZ

What skill of Molly's did Ann and the docent admire?
ⓐ her ability to draw
ⓑ her effort to practice

KEY WORDS

- inspire
- inner
- lean over
- life-sized

- figure
- typical
- garb (= clothes)
- poke

- snap a picture of
- sparkling
- upturned
- familiar

Ann snapped a picture of Molly, her eyes sparkling and her lips slightly upturned.

"You didn't smile," said Ann. She showed her the picture on her cell phone.

"It's my Renaissance smile. Remember Mona Lisa?"

"By Leonardo da Vinci," replied Ann. "Of course. It's only the most famous painting of the period. Will you take my picture now?"

The girls turned back towards the figures and a familiar face smiled back at them. "Hannah!" they cried.

"Surprised to see me?" asked Hannah.

Ann and Molly nodded through giggles. "Where have you
been?" asked Molly. "We've been on every floor of the
museum today. A letter came to my house—"

"About finding your heart's desire," said Hannah. "Well,"
she smiled. "Did you find it?"

"Uh… I…" stammered Molly, confused. "How did you know
about the letter?"

"I sent it," said Hannah.

"*You*?" Ann and Molly looked at each other. Now they were
even *more* confused.

"My cousin works at the information desk," replied Hannah.

"The woman who gave us the envelope?" asked Ann.

"But she acted like she didn't know anything about it!"

"She's the one who helped me," said Hannah. "She told me about the Renaissance exhibit here at the Huntingdon and I knew it would be a great resource for our school project. So we planned a quest so you could gather information."

POP QUIZ

Who told Hannah about the Renaissance exhibit at the museum?

ⓐ Ann and Molly

ⓑ her cousin working at the museum

KEY WORDS

▪ stammer   ▪ confused   ▪ resource

"All of the people at the museum were in on your plan, I suppose," said Molly. Hannah smiled and nodded. "Did you have fun, exploring the Renaissance?"

"Oh, yes," said Molly. "And we learned so much about the period! Who knew the fourteenth, fifteenth, and sixteenth centuries could be so fascinating? But what was the idea about finding my heart's desire?"

"I just had a feeling that you might like one of the floors more than the others."

Ann suddenly grabbed Molly's arm. "Molly! The look on your face when you were sketching. You loved everything to do with the fourth floor fashions!"

Molly didn't miss the twinkle in Hannah's eye.

POP QUIZ

What did Hannah think was Molly's heart's desire?

ⓐ music and art

ⓑ clothes and fashion

"But I haven't ever shown you my sketchbook," said Molly. "I've been keeping that a secret!"

Hannah laughed. "Your interest in fashion is not much of a secret when you talk about clothes and fashion *all the time*."

Molly and Ann laughed, too. "I've never been very good at keeping secrets from my best friends," said Molly.

She paused, the smile slipping off her face. "But what about both of you? Will you be happy working on a project about Renaissance clothing?"

Hannah and Ann nodded their eager approval.

POP QUIZ

Which topic did the girls agree to work on together?

ⓐ Renaissance painting
ⓑ Renaissance clothing

KEY WORDS

- to do with
- twinkle
- keep A a secret (keep-kept-kept)
- be not much of
- be good at

- keep secrets
- slip off
- eager
- approval

"There are plenty of interesting facts about the styles in those days," said Ann. "Did you know that women wanted to be blonde, even back then? I'll investigate hair and shoes."
"And look at this long list of fashion terms," said Hannah. "Don't you want to know what a leg-of-mutton sleeve is? Or pumpkin hose? I'll do the research and you can do the sketches."
"It's always better when you love the topic you're working on, right?" asked Molly.
"Absolutely," said Ann and Hannah, arm in arm with Molly.

▲ leg-of-mutton sleeve

▲ pumpkin hose

KEY WORDS

- **plenty of** (= a lot of / lots of)
- term
- leg-of-mutton sleeve
- pumpkin hose
- arm in arm with
- fabulous

The girls started down the long, marble staircase, chatting
excitedly about the project.

"Thanks, Hannah," said Ann, when they'd reached the first
floor. "This was the most fun I've ever had working on a
school project!"

"I'll say," said Molly. "And thank *you*, Huntingdon
Museum of Art. You were fabulous, darling!"

A Mark T for true or F for false.

❶ Molly and Ann were allowed to touch the clothes on the fourth floor. T F

❷ Hannah's cousin was a docent who worked on the fourth floor. T F

❸ Hannah thought the Renaissance exhibit would be a great resource for their project. T F

❹ Molly couldn't find her heart's desire at the end of her quest. T F

B Match each thing with the right explanation.

❶ perfume ·

❷ stockings ·

❸ farthingales ·

· a) tightly fitted to show off a man's legs

· b) masked body odor and the smell of clothing

· c) grew so big that laws were made to limit them

C Choose the best answer to each question.

❶ Which of the following statements is NOT true?

   a) During the Renaissance, men wore colorful tights.

   b) Women wore veils or hats to show off their wealth.

   c) Men wore a tight-fitting coat called a "doublet."

   d) The actor playing Romeo wore a doublet in the movie, *Romeo and Juliet*.

❷ How did Hannah know what Molly's heart's desire was?

   a) Hannah had read Molly's diary.

   b) Hannah had overheard Molly tell Ann.

   c) Hannah had found Molly's secret sketchbook.

   d) Molly talked about fashion and clothes all the time.

D Connect each character with what each character is supposed to do.

❶ Molly   •   • a) doing the research about fashion terms

❷ Hannah •   • b) doing the sketches of clothes

❸ Ann   •   • c) investigating hair and shoes

Let's Review the Story

Fill in the blanks to review the story.

❶ **Title:** _____ at the _____

❷ **The Main Characters and What They Want:**
Molly wants to find her h_____ d_____.
Ann wants to work on the R_____ project that their teacher has assigned.
Hannah wants her friends to come to the Huntingdon Museum of Art and follow the c_____ of the q_____.

❸ **What Molly and Ann Did in the Huntingdon Museum:**
On the second floor, the girls discovered interesting i_____ from the Renaissance and different styles of singing like polyphony and m_____. On the third floor, they found hundreds of great i_____, and most importantly, the p_____ p_____. On the fourth floor, they learned how f_____ t_____ developed during the Renaissance.

❹ **How the Quest Helped the Characters:**
After s_____ Renaissance dresses, Molly understood that f_____ was her heart desire.
Ann found all kinds of i_____ that would help her with the Renaissance project.
Hannah is glad to have helped Molly find her heart's desire.
The girls are all happy to have Renaissance fashions as the t_____ of their school project.

Let's Think & Talk

Think about the following questions and answer them freely.

❶ Imagine you could visit the Huntingdon Museum. Tell us what floor you would want to look around first.

❷ If you were Hannah, imagine how you would deliver clues and messages to Molly.

❸ If you did a project about the Renaissance, in what area would you want to research and make a presentation about?

❹ What is your "heart's desire"?

Let's Review the Story

❶ Title: Mystery at the Museum

❷ **The Main Characters and What They Want:**

Molly wants to find her heart's desire.

Ann wants to work on the Renaissance project that their teacher has assigned.

Hannah wants her friends to come to the Huntingdon Museum of Art and follow the clues of the quest.

❸ **What Molly and Ann Did in the Huntingdon Museum:**

On the second floor, the girls discovered interesting instruments from the Renaissance and different styles of singing like polyphony and madrigals. On the third floor, they found hundreds of great inventions, and most importantly, the printing press. On the fourth floor, they learned how fashion trends developed during the Renaissance.

❹ **How the Quest Helped the Characters:**

After sketching Renaissance dresses, Molly understood that fashion was her heart desire.

Ann found all kinds of information that would help her with the Renaissance project.

Hannah is glad to have helped Molly find her heart's desire.

The girls are all happy to have Renaissance fashions as the topic of their school project.

Smart Readers: **Wise** & **Wide**

After-reading **Test**

- Mystery at the Museum
- Level 5
- 29 Questions

(Vocabulary 6 / Reading Comprehension 16 /

Sentence Structure & Grammar 7)

1. Which pair has the wrong past tense form of the verb?
   ① sing – sung   ② rinse – rinsed
   ③ shrug – shruged   ④ shake – shook

2. Which of the following has the closest meaning with the word "quest"?
   ① plan   ② search
   ③ clue   ④ display

3. What is "calligraphy"?
   ① decorative writing
   ② a rainbow of colors
   ③ signs for the museum
   ④ pictures of famous people

4. Who is a "docent"?
   ① a director of a gallery
   ② a museum volunteer
   ③ a staff member of a theater
   ④ an assistant teacher

5. Which is the correct meaning of "skim" in the following sentence?

   "He didn't invent it," said Molly, skimming the information.

   ① to watch something very carefully
   ② to read something quickly
   ③ to move quickly over a surface
   ④ to look for a person or thing

6. Choose the common word for the two blanks.

> • A tangle of excitement zipped _____ her.
> • The player flipped _____ the music on his stand.

① on   ② into
③ out   ④ through

7. What was the subject of the project that the girls had to do?
① European history
② The Renaissance
③ Great inventions
④ Scientific Method

8. What did the girls find on the doorstep after they heard a knock?
① a note for Hannah
② an envelope with Molly's name on it
③ a love letter from a secret admirer
④ Molly's notebook

9. Why did the letter say, "Do not delay!"?
① The girls would not be able to solve the mystery after lunch.
② The museum was free to the public, but they had to enter before 12:00.
③ The museum was only open on weekdays and it was Friday.
④ The girls had to solve the quest within the day.

10. Why did Molly introduce herself to the employee at the information desk?
① She thought she recognized the woman at the desk.
② She wondered if the employee had a clue for her.
③ She wanted to make a new friend in the museum.
④ She was not sure that the woman knew her and Ann.

11. What could the girls find out more about on the second floor?

    ① old buildings

    ② astronomy

    ③ musical notes

    ④ printing and type

12. How did the girls listen to the instruments on the second floor?

    ① by using their cell phones

    ② by putting on the headphones

    ③ by playing the instruments by themselves

    ④ by touching the plaques beside the instruments

13. Which statement about the composer, Jacques Arcadelt, is NOT true?

    ① He was one of the most famous and influential composers of madrigals.

    ② His works were performed during the early period of the Dark Ages.

    ③ His works were considered classics.

    ④ The publication of his first book helped spread madrigal music throughout Europe.

14. Why did the lute player suddenly hand a letter to Molly?

    ① He heard Ann say Molly's name.

    ② Molly asked if he had a message for her.

    ③ The docent told him to give Molly the letter.

    ④ The letter suddenly fell off his music stand.

15. What phrases in the letter led the girls to the third floor?

    ① "scientific thinking" and "keep searching"

    ② "people experimented" and "music and instruments"

    ③ "fashion trends" and "threaded with silver and gold"

    ④ "gossip magazines" and "the printing press"

16. Who was responsible for revolutionizing the process of printing?
    ① Leonardo da Vinci
    ② Galileo Galilei
    ③ Johannes Gutenberg
    ④ Filippo Brunelleschi

17. What modern day invention did Molly compare to the printing press?
    ① newspapers
    ② radio
    ③ the Internet
    ④ smartphones

18. Why was the Scientific Method so important during the Renaissance?
    ① It developed during the period and disappeared.
    ② It helped people realize the artistic aspects of life.
    ③ It encouraged scientists to take detailed notes.
    ④ It led to controlled experiments and the analysis of data.

19. Who believed that the Earth rotated around the sun? Choose two answers.
    ① Michelangelo
    ② Galileo
    ③ Copernicus
    ④ Shakespeare

20. Why was it so important for Molly to find her heart's desire on the fourth floor?
    ① The museum was about to close.
    ② She had a strong expectation.
    ③ The clues she had were crucial.
    ④ The fourth floor was the last floor.

21. Why did Molly refuse to smile in the cutout figure?
    ① She was angry with Ann for taking her picture.
    ② She was copying the smile from *the Mona Lisa*.
    ③ She saw something strange in the room.
    ④ She didn't like the clothes the woman wore.

22. Why did Hannah send the girls on a quest at the Huntingdon Museum?
    ① She wanted to find her heart's desire at the museum.
    ② She hates doing online research for a project.
    ③ She likes doing a project of her favorite topic.
    ④ She knew that there was an exhibit about the Renaissance there.

※ Choose the correct sentence. (23~24)
23. ① A well-dressed woman tapped Molly on the shoulder.
    ② A well-dressed woman tapped her on Molly's shoulder.
    ③ A well-dressed woman tapped to Molly's shoulder.
    ④ A well-dressed woman tapped the shoulder on Molly.

24. ① Molly has kept that being secrets.
    ② Molly has been keeping secrets that.
    ③ Molly has been keeping that a secret.
    ④ Molly has been keeping a secret of that.

※ Choose the wrong part of each sentence. (25~26)
25.
Renaissance ladies would have fit in nice in a vampire movie!
             ①   ②   ③   ④

26.

The <u>wealth</u> used <u>clothing</u> to establish <u>their</u> position <u>in</u> society.
     ①   ②   ③   ④

※ Choose the correct word(s) for each blank. (27~29)

27.

She had no idea _____ to search next.

① that   ② where
③ while   ④ as

28.

If _____ I had a Gutenberg Bible, I'd be rich!

① far   ② just
③ only   ④ very

29.

_____ we start on this project, _____ we can finish.

① The soon, sooner   ② Sooner, the soonest
③ The sooner, the sooner   ④ The soonest, the soon

Memo

Memo

Memo

Memo

Cathy C. Hall

Cathy C. Hall graduated with a broadcasting degree, working in the radio industry as a news reporter and commercial copywriter before going back to school to earn English certification. She spent a decade in education, teaching preschoolers, middle schoolers, and high schoolers. Now, she's a full-time freelance writer, with stories, essays, and poems in publications for both children and adults. Her byline appears in books like *Uncle John's Facts To Annoy Your Teacher, Chicken Soup for the Soul's Think Positive for Kids, Cup of Comfort for Dog Lovers*, and many more. She lives near Atlanta, Georgia, with her husband and a miniature dachshund.

 5-5

Mystery at the Museum

Written by Cathy C. Hall
Illustrated by Juyeong Lee

First Published in October 2015

Editorial Manager: Juyon Choi
Editors: Juyon Choi, Nayoung Seo, Kyunghee Jang, Jiyeong Park
Designers: Eunhee Lee, Elim
Cover Designer: Eunhee Lee

Published and distributed by

 Happy House

Darakwon Bldg., 64-1 Jandari-ro, Mapo-gu, Seoul, Korea 04031
Tel: 82-2-736-2031(ext. 250)   Fax: 82-2-732-2037
Homepage: www.ihappyhouse.co.kr
Publisher: Kyudo Chung

Copyright © Darakwon Publishing Company 2015
English Edition published 2015, by arrangement with Darakwon, by Happy House
English Edition Copyright © 2015, Happy House

ISBN: 978-89-6653-206-3 18740 / 978-89-6653-156-1 18740(set)

[Components]
• 1 Audio CD (Recording Studio: Aram)
• Answer Keys & Korean Translation: Free download at www.ihappyhouse.co.kr